SPEAK THE WORD!
Seven Scriptures to Take Your Life Back!

KHAIRIYA C. BRYANT

All Scripture quotations, unless otherwise indicated, are taken from the Holy Bible, New International Version®, NIV®. Copyright ©1973, 1978, 1984, 2011 by Biblica, Inc.™ Used by permission of Zondervan. All rights reserved worldwide. www.zondervan.com The "NIV" and "New International Version" are trademarks registered in the United States Patent and Trademark Office by Biblica, Inc.™

Scripture quotations marked (CEV) are from the Contemporary English Version Copyright © 1991, 1992, 1995 by American Bible Society, Used by Permission.

Scripture quotations marked MSG are taken from THE MESSAGE, copyright © 1993, 1994, 1995, 1996, 2000, 2001, 2002 by Eugene H. Peterson. Used by permission of NavPress. All rights reserved. Represented by Tyndale House Publishers, Inc.

Scripture taken from the New King James Version®. Copyright © 1982 by Thomas Nelson. Used by permission. All rights reserved.

Scripture quotations marked (TLB) are taken from The Living Bible copyright © 1971. Used by permission of Tyndale House Publishers, Inc., Carol Stream, Illinois 60188. All rights reserved.

Scriptures marked KJV are taken from the KING JAMES VERSION (KJV): KING JAMES VERSION, public domain.

Scriptures marked ESV are taken from THE HOLY BIBLE ENGLISH STANDARD VERSION ® Copywrite© 2001 by Crossway; a publishing ministry of Good News Publishers. Used by Permission.

DEDICATION

To the storm and the wind. To the tears and the strength
of my heart. To the voice of God inside, constantly
keeping conscious, every shortfall and triumph.
You are not alone.

CONTENTS

ACKNOWLEDGMENTS

Thank you, God, for the lesson in the blessing. I could cry every day from the joy I have experienced getting to know you in my low places.

Thank you, Twin for never allowing me to be alone in the spiritual or physical. You are my forever-sister, my twin-flame, my soul-mate.

Thank you, Magnificent Seven:
Atiya; Jasmin; Tahirah; Taj-Malik; Ian-Isaiah; Zakhai-Nasir; and Khairiya Kelis Amani, for giving me my most important lessons in unconditional love. You are my proof that God trusted me.

Thank you, Charles M. Bryant, III for the cover graphics.

Mommy, I love you!

Daddy and MaMa, Rest in Power, and keep protecting me.

INTRODUCTION

We walk by faith and not by sight. But many times we feel like we are left alone in the darkness to figure out for ourselves, not only how we got to THIS place, but how we are going to get out. When we are less than able to decipher the necessary tools for survival, let alone improvement, what do we do?

I wasn't always in tune with my spirit. I allowed my earthly, mindful self to make the decisions for me. Because of that, many of my decisions were based on shear emotion, and not on what was spiritually best for my soul to move forward in the likeness of Christ. Please, do not get me wrong – I am not THERE yet, wherever there tends to be. I am trying daily to live my best spiritual life guided by the fact that God LOVES me like no one else ever will. Initially, that love never seemed like enough, but as I hope you will see through these pages, God and His guidance is all you will ever need to live a best-case-scenario-life.

With God, you have an opportunity to tame your emotional responses to the stimuli that hits us every morning, the second we are blessed enough to open our eyes, and get out of our beds. Yes, a blessing it is to face the world with its myriad of concerns, conceits, and curve balls. But we can live a fruitful life despite our difficulties. Wherever you are, if you are focused on a life of love and light, you can take control of your emotions, and take your life back!

1 MAKE LOVE YOUR LIGHT

SCRIPTURE 1: 9. Anyone who claims to be in the light but hates a brother or sister is still in darkness. 10. Anyone who loves their brother and sister lives in the light and there is nothing in them to make them stumble. 11. But anyone who hates his brother or sister is in the darkness and walks around in the darkness. They do not know where they are going, because the darkness has blinded them. 1 John 2:9-11 (NIV).

What can cause us the most pain? Our relationships! How do we relate one to another? When we interact with the people in our lives—whether we have chosen them through marriage or other similar connections, or we have not chosen them, by birth, workplace, or even school—if the interaction is anything less than positive in our perception, we open ourselves to a myriad of negative emotions: hurt; anger; pain; vengeance; discontent; resentment; contempt; envy; jealousy; humiliation; faithlessness; apathy; hostility; spitefulness. Have you ever found yourself visiting any of those emotional stand-stills? If you have, it is likely that you feel powerless to move your life forward and allow past hurts to be healed. When we are stuck in negative emotional spaces, we lack control over our lives. To take our lives back, we must realize how we perceive our relationships and then seek to interact from a spiritual place first.

When a relationship is good, it is great! But when it is not so good, it is horrible. As people, we tend to equate things on both ends – the good is always "better" and the bad is always "worse" than either reality. That is an equalized emotional balance. But as soon as we make an opportunity to step back, we find the good was a lot less covered in gold, and the bad stopped far shorter than representing the dirt on the bottom of our shoe.

1 John 2:9-10 gives us a template for how to balance our perceptions in all relationships when it states, *9. If we claim to be in the light and hate someone, we are still in the dark." 10. But if we love others, we are in the light, and we don't cause problems for them.* (CEV). There is a balance among persons that will be established in any relationship. This balance will move like a see-saw or a pendulum in accordance with where the relationship is moving, and may even allow us the opportunity to nudge the relationship into a better place. There may always be a time when one person appears to have the upper hand, but whichever position you find yourself in now, staying in the light will help you take back your life.

What does it mean to be in the light, and why do I want to be there?

In the general sense, "light" can mean being knowledgeable or enlightened. We have a well-informed outlook; we are aware; we are educated; open-minded; and wise. In a spiritual sense, when we walk in the light, we take all the objectives listed, and apply them to our dealings with, and our intentions toward, other people.

To walk in the light, I must be knowledgeable about myself. Who am I as a person in this moment of the interaction, and what am I bringing to the table? Am I aware of my current emotional state? Am I happy or sad, angry or joyful, content or feeling inadequate? Whatever your emotional state, it is important that you have a sense for where you are so that you can be mindful of the basis for your responses to the stimulus of another person.

For example, if I have had a particularly difficult day, and I've felt overlooked, and I later offer my assistance to someone, and she tells me she doesn't need my help, I may feel rejected and then internalize what she said to mean that she does not love or care about me, because she will not accept my offer. In reality, the person just doesn't need any help at that time, and that is okay. If I am aware that I am off balance in my feelings, then I will not react negatively simply because my offer was not accepted. Or, if I do feel negatively, I have a chance to dial back my emotional response, and tap into my spiritual response, which is to offer "love" by walking in the light.

Walking in the light means being willing to look within yourself before reacting to another person's "negative" actions. Walking in the light means not perceiving another person's actions as negative, but simply "accepting" their actions toward you, are their best effort at the time. Being in the light means that we must assume that people are operating at their highest level of capability at that time, and to the extent that they fall short, we must give them grace. In 1 John 1:5-7, John explains: *5. This is the message we have heard from him and proclaim to you, that God is light, and in him is no darkness at all. 6. If we say we have fellowship with him while we walk in darkness, we lie and do not practice the truth. 7. But if we walk in the light, as he is in the light, we have fellowship with one another, and the blood of Jesus his Son cleanses us from all sin.* (English Standard Version)

Because Jesus is, we can be the light of our world. In Hebrews 12:2, we are told to live our lives with our eyes fixed on the light (Jesus). Jesus is the example for us to follow. *When Jesus spoke to the people again he said "I am the light of the world. Whoever follows me will never walk in darkness, but will have the light of life."* John 8:12 (NIV). When Peter focused on Jesus, he was able to walk on water. When he began to focus on the waves, he began to sink and had to call out to Jesus for help. Matthew 14:22-23. When we focus on the light instead of the darkness, we are better equipped to rise above our issues.

In modern day, what does it mean to walk on the water? In essence, it means that you have the capacity to rise above any and all circumstances. In order to take our lives back from whatever or whoever holds us hostage, we must have enough faith to believe that we already contain within ourselves everything we need to rise above the situation, when we stay focused on the Light. It does not matter if you see the light as an actual illumination of your best qualities and responses to negativity, or if you choose to characterize it as the Christ living within you. Your outcome will be the same.

Many times when I have recognized that I was "operating in the light," I would clarify it as my "God-response," because I would have reacted very differently. One glaring example happened the first time I realized that God speaks to me through the Word:

***

I was going through a particularly difficult time with my now ex-husband. We had not spoken to one another for close to three days. On this evening (the night that Prince William and Kate were married), my ex came into the room where I was watching a show on the television and started talking to me about the program. It was a little awkward, and completely out of the blue, because we had not spoken in three days. After a short conversation, he left the bedroom and went into the living room. I fell asleep, but awakened around 12:00 in the morning, hungry and searching for pretzels in the kitchen. It was then that I noticed the house was uncharacteristically dark. There were no lights on in the living room, and no lights on in the den. I walked around the house looking for my ex and he was nowhere to be found. I checked outside, and the car was still in the driveway. I began to call his cell phone which rang but went unanswered. Somewhere around three in the morning, he answered and told me that he was on a bus on his way to North Carolina. From experience, I knew he had a female "friend" in the state, and I assumed that was his destination. My marriage was officially over.

My level of anger that morning was such that I knew only God could get me back down to a point of acceptance and calm, so that I could function at work and at home. I searched for a passage of scripture that I had relied on in the past. Before I started keeping a journal, I had a brown napkin where I scribbled scripture, and for the life of me, I could not find the scripture I thought I needed on that napkin. Instead, I got this:

Ephesians 4:31-32 Get rid of all bitterness, rage and anger, brawling and slander, along with every form of malice. 32. Be kind and compassionate to one another, forgiving each other, just as Christ forgave you. (NIV)

In the moment, I had no intention to forgive him – I was looking for a scripture just to calm my nerves – but I imagine God gave me what He knew I needed at the time, to do what I was going to be called to do. After several days, my ex called home and told me that he wanted to return, but he had no money and needed me to buy him a ticket. I refused, laughed hysterically, and hung up the phone – not my finest moment. He continued to call back and pleaded with me to get him a ticket. I was now sitting in the catbird seat with no desire to send him any money.

I called my mother to give her the specifics, and cackled through every sentence. When I finished speaking with her, I felt a sense of calm, but more than that, I felt a sense of superiority. But it was now Sunday, and I couldn't go to church feeling contempt for my spouse. I went back to my Bible before I left for service. It opened "randomly" to Proverbs 24:17-18: *Do not gloat when your enemy falls; when they stumble, do not let your heart rejoice, 18. or the LORD will see and disapprove and turn his wrath away from them.* (NIV) To say I was taken aback would be an understatement. I was outright afraid that God spoke to me so clearly through his Word. To compound my fear, the sermon that day focused on being obedient to God's Word, once heard.

So, after I was told to get rid of my bitterness, rage, anger and malice, and to forgive; to stop gloating and be obedient; I agreed to send the money and prayed in preparation for his return. My typical practice at that time was to pray and then read scripture. The scripture I received after prayer was 2 Corinthians 2:5-11:
5. If anyone has caused grief, he has not so much grieved me as he has grieved all of you to some extent—not to put it too severely. 6. The punishment inflicted on him by the majority is sufficient. 7. Now instead, you ought to forgive and comfort him, so that he will not be overwhelmed by excessive sorrow. 8. I urge you, therefore, to reaffirm your love for him. 9. Another reason I wrote you was to see if you would stand the test and be obedient in everything. 10. Anyone you forgive, I also forgive. And what I have forgiven—if there was anything to forgive—I have forgiven in the sight of Christ for your

sake, 11. in order that Satan might not outwit us. For we are not unaware of his schemes.

Nothing inside of me wanted to let my ex come back home, let alone help him to get there, but I was honestly afraid when God "spoke" to me in this manner. The next scripture from my napkin said this: *Do not take revenge, my dear friends, but leave room for God's wrath, for it is written: "It is mine to avenge; I will repay," says the Lord. 20. On the contrary: "If your enemy is hungry, feed him; if he is thirsty, give him something to drink. In doing this, you will heap burning coals on his head."* Romans 12:19-20. (NIV) Ultimately, it was not my flesh response, but my God-response (and a healthy dose of God-fearing) that allowed him the opportunity to come back home. I purchased the ticket and he arrived.

***

Eventually, what we should aspire to is no longer being able to recognize a separation between our flesh-response and our God-response. When that happens, we know that our spirit is leading our mind and our bodies. That is the epitome of the Light!

In a very practical sense, walking in the light means being willing to live your life in accordance to Jesus' example. Jesus said, *38. "You have heard that it was said, 'Eye for eye, and tooth for tooth. 39. But I tell you, do not resist an evil person. If anyone slaps you on the right cheek, turn to them the other cheek also."* Matthew 5:38-39 (NIV). So, if we are not paying back petty behavior for petty behavior, and we know that vengeance belongs to the Lord, how is it that we are supposed to turn the other cheek, give up our cloak, and go one extra mile beyond the one we didn't want to take in the first place?

If we are to attempt to walk in the light of who Jesus would have us to be, we are going to have to ask and answer for ourselves several different questions:

What does it mean to turn the other cheek?

What happens when we run out of cheeks?

How difficult is it to make ourselves vulnerable so that we emulate Jesus more and more?

What does it mean to have a renewed mind in Christ?

In my walk with God, as I've built a stronger relationship with Him, I've found my spiritual connection (wanting to do good) stronger at times when I know someone "deserves" my wrath. I have come to a point where I can extend them an opportunity to do better by me. Part of this is that my heart is convicted and wants to do right. The other portion of this, is realizing that I need to extend grace to my human counterparts just as God extends grace to us.

In order to be forgiven by God, we first must be able to forgive others. Matthew 6:15. God says we must forgive one another seventy times seven – this is the epitome of grace. Matthew 18:22. Grace is when God gives you another opportunity to be forgiven of your sins, knowing that everything about your actions were wrong, wrong, wrong – whether purposefully so, or not.

Grace isn't something that we have to earn. It is a "gimmie" from God. Grace is the love God continues to show us even when (especially when) we are in our worst possible states: when we are right a little or wrong a lot, God continues to love and cherish us. Each day that we awaken, we get brand new grace and mercy. Lamentations 3:22-23.

It is not always easy to extend grace to people who have done us a disservice, or simply do not like us for a petty reason or no reason at all. It remains very uncomfortable to our mind when we feel we are being taken advantage of; but can anyone really take advantage of our emotions and feelings? At first, we might think 'yes,' but in all honesty, if we truly look at the situation and no physical disadvantage is realized, what have we lost by loving someone through extending grace? Yes, there are times when love requires action, and many will tell you that love is an action word, but loving someone enough to extend grace through forgiveness is a winning action just for you!

Loving someone through grace is "simply" saying to yourself: "I am not going to hold their negative behavior against them." Making that decision for yourself frees you to move forward past another person's actions, and not allow it to hold you emotionally captive. This is a key step to taking back your life: Love yourself enough to let go; or love the offender enough to let go; or love God enough to let go!

How best to handle this may come to you in either way, or a combination of the three. To take your life back, you must confront at least one of the three reasons. Then, you will have to make a choice to love. Make love your light and take your life back!

2 WHAT'S LOVE GOT TO DO WITH IT?

What's love got to do with it? Everything, everything, everything! Love is what we are called to do – Love is what Jesus did for us when he went to the cross – God showed how much he loved us when He sent Jesus to die for us.

Love saves us from ourselves! We are commanded to love God with all our heart, all our soul and all our strength, (Deut. 6:5) and with all our mind, as well. (Luke 10:27, Mark 12:30, Matt. 22:37) We are commanded to love our neighbors as we love ourselves, and then advised that there is no commandment greater than these. Mark 12:31. Men are called to love their wives as they love and care for themselves, for who would not take care of his own body? (Ephesians 5:28-30).

Of course, this assumes first that you have found yourself worthy to love. I know many people struggle with self-love and acceptance, and this text won't necessarily address this very important issue. However, if you find yourself stuck in a place where you may not be able to fully love yourself, think about the feeling you get when you help another person. Even on our worst emotional days, when we find an opportunity to assist another person, and make that person feel good, the action of helping can immediately change our perspective and lighten our hearts; if only for a moment. By loving others – even when we love ourselves less than we should – we can move from a dark emotional space into the light by giving light, and extending grace.

Now that we know that love is required, what kind of love are we talking about? You may know that there are three (some say four) types of love: eros; phileo; and agape. Even if you didn't know that, you certainly know the emotional connections that are attached to at least two of the three. Eros is explained as romantic love. It is the feeling that two people have for each other that is based on attraction, romance and chemistry. It is the love that drives relationships of a sexual nature. Phileo is the type of love you have for a family member or a close friend who you see as a brother or sister. There are no romantic feelings attached to this type of love. Agape love is probably the most unfamiliar, and one that you may not have yet come across. Agape love is the type of love that God has for us as His children. It is the type of love that Jesus showed for us when he went to the cross and died for our sin. It is also the type of love that God commands us to have towards our neighbors. Unlike eros and phileo, agape love is not based on feelings. Agape love is what it truly means to extend grace – loving someone whether we feel it emotionally or not. Agape love is the type of love that is explained in 1 Corinthians 13. It is the kind of love we hear recited at many wedding ceremonies, but couples often find lacking in the actual marriage:

4. Love is kind and patient, never jealous, boastful, proud, or 5 rude. Love isn't selfish or quick tempered. It doesn't keep a record of wrongs that others do. 6 Love rejoices in the truth, but not in evil. 7.

Love is always supportive, loyal, hopeful, and trusting. 8 Love never fails! (CEV)

The Biblical concept of love is not based on emotions. The concept reflects a set of values that when applied, represents the type of actions that God wants us to show to ourselves and to others. A major part of taking your life back is being able to apply Biblical love as self-love, and then in all other circumstances. Be gentle with your love and acceptance of self, so that you can be gentle with others, and extend the grace required to live in the light.

If you are still having a difficult time grasping this concept, try this: Think about the best romantic relationship you've ever had – regardless of how it ended, or if it continues in a lesser form than when it started. Think back to the time when you were infatuated with the person and just falling in love. Your thoughts stayed focused on that person. When he or she was out of your presence, you wanted to know that he or she was okay. Sometimes the thought of them gave you butterflies, and you couldn't imagine life without that person. You called and connected for no reason other than to hear that person's voice. Are you there? Great. When you are in that phase of romantic love, your brain shuts off – and every indecision, red flag, mistake that person makes gets washed away by the *feelings* you have for him or her, and your desire to keep that person in your circle and close to your heart. Your willingness to give that person the benefit of the doubt, even when every realistic option says otherwise, is the extension of grace and love we need to have for all people in our lives – whether they are momentary (at a traffic light, the job or school) or perennial (the one you married, your parents, children, siblings, etc.).

Loving one another in this manner will keep us out of the darkness, and keep us from wandering around aimless and blind. Some people believe that being vulnerable to love in this way sets us up for victimization, but loving in this manner not only allows us to operate outside of iniquity, it also disarms the "enemy." When we operate outside of love, when we hate our brother or sister in the world, our actions tend to reflect those feelings. We may harbor resentment and then act out that resentment on a non-suspecting and undeserving party.

Think back on how many times you raised your voice at an unsuspecting person (friend, spouse, child, or stranger), simply because you were carrying around anger for another person. For myself, I know that I would never spank my children if they were misbehaving during a time when I was upset with their father. I feared that if I spanked them in that moment, the discipline would not come from a place of love and correction, but from a place of darkness and anger, and they would receive something that wasn't intended for them.

Many women, including myself, have suffered through and survived a violent domestic relationship to varying degrees. What anyone knows who has been through that situation is that nothing the woman did or said warranted that man's behavior, or was vaguely related or relevant to any action performed or not performed. But only because the male participant lacked love for himself, he operated outside of the light, in darkness, and was blinded by his "hatred" for the real reason for his behavior – someone in his past who also operated in darkness. Offering grace – not harboring hatred and discontent for the one who "wronged" you – allows you to rise above your circumstances, and prevents your current situation from dictating a future negative action.

Light is love. There is no other way to ensure that you are not walking in the darkness and aimlessly through life. Think about the darkness of vengeance, which is a direct reflection of a lack of love for yourself, as well as your target. Why? Negativity breeds negativity. Whether you believe in the law of attraction; the law of sowing and reaping; or the law of karma, whatever you put out is what you are going to get back. If you spend your time fashioning defenses, or even worse, devising offenses, you have given your life over to the offender, and are preventing yourself from moving your life forward. In addition, you are creating future negative responses and consequences for those vengeful acts.

There was a time when I had the best professional job of my life. It was an appellate attorney position working for the state. All I did was research and write briefs and prepare to argue specialized issues of law before a three-judge panel. I traveled across the state on a regular basis and had the freedom to take vacation and sick days as needed. The pay wasn't great, but the benefits were amazing, and I really loved the subject matter. However, I am a very independent worker, and my supervisor was a micro-manager.

In the beginning, it mattered little because I was new to the position and I wanted and needed to learn. But as I became better at the job, the supervisor began to pay closer and closer attention to my work, and make what I believed were unnecessary changes to my work product. The straw that broke this camel's back was when she insisted that I use the word "present" for "current," for no reason other than "present" was the word choice that she preferred. But her name was not on the document, it was mine. There were rarely any corrections to the legal analysis or arguments – to which I gladly accepted correction. We had several heated discussions, and going forward, I went to sleep thinking bad thoughts about my supervisor, and I woke up thinking bad thoughts about my supervisor. My stomach remained in knots throughout the day and the stress began to show in my work product. Eventually I stopped caring about the work and cared more about preparing my defenses for when the supervisor approached me with more "petty" corrections.

Not only did focusing on my supervisor's negativity stagnate my thought process, but being unable to love her through and past her own shortcomings completely changed the trajectory of my professional life. I wanted nothing less than to become the Solicitor General for the state of Florida and argue before the United States Supreme Court. Because I operated in darkness – even though I did nothing wrong to her – I became blinded to my future; became aimless in my approach to the situation; and stagnated my own life when I quit! It was a lesson well learned.

God does not want you to be mistreated. God does not want you to be victimized. But God does want you to make all choices from a starting point within the light. Your best decisions will always be made from a point of illumination. Illuminate the situation, and then illuminate your response to the situation. Choose to operate in love and light and you will be able to clearly decide how to move yourself from darkness and take back your life!

There is something to be said about the saying: "kill them with kindness." Eventually, even the most difficult devil in your life will leave you alone when there is no longer any "fun" attached to your offering grace, love and light to their negative behaviors. *The thief comes only to steal and kill and destroy.* John 10:10 (NIV). If he can't take enough from you to make you act the fool; stomp; pout; lash out physically or verbally; or conspire to negativity, you will take away the power you gave to him and take your life back at the same time!

3 MAKE YOUR DEMONS SUBMIT

SCRIPTURE 2: The seventy-two returned with joy and said, "Lord, even the demons submit to us in your name." Luke 10:17 (NIV).

Taking back your life necessarily includes disarming your enemy. This may be a person, but it may also be your addiction to a negative behavior or habit. It may be very obvious to you who your enemies might be, but it is equally important to determine what inanimate enemies (or your reaction to them) are causing you to stumble, or preventing you from moving your life forward. This step will require you to take inventory of your life. Whatever it is that holds you back from being your best presentation of self, must submit in the name of Jesus!

In 1 John 2:15, we are commanded - *Don't love the world or anything that belongs to the world.* (CEV) But what does it mean to love the world? Many of us would choose to believe that as long as we are not materialistic, we have no love for worldly things. True enough, it is easy to spot our own materialism when we have that trait, but love of the world can be very subtle. In fact, love of the world could manifest itself by showing a lack of love for God.

We show a lack of love for God by not finding time in our lives to create a relationship with Him through reading the Bible, studying scripture, prayer, and worship. As a woman, it is very important to me that my significant other show me in some way that he loves me. If he spends no time with me; if he doesn't at least know my favorite color; if he has no insight into the foods that make me the happiest to consume, I will assume he doesn't love me because he did not care enough to take the time to learn me. I may even decide that this relationship is no longer worth my time and energy. I may then move on.

Although I don't want to suggest that God will move away from you if you don't show your love for Him by learning and living His Word to your best ability, I will go so far as to say, not having a relationship with God, will keep you from being able to fully access his promises, and achieve your true blessings. You can't use it, if you don't know *how* to use it.

Being a lover of worldly things prevents us from keeping the Word of Christ. When we choose our personal life preferences and comfort to the exclusion of building our relationship with God, by filling or fulfilling ourselves with any person or thing instead of the Holy Spirit, we cannot perfect our lives and move it forward. To be our best spiritual selves, we must abide in the enjoyment of what God loves and make that the object of our pursuit. 1 John 2:5-6 *But whoever keeps His word, truly the love of God is perfected in him. By this we know that we are in Him. 6 He who says he abides in Him ought himself also to walk just as He walked.* (NIV).

When we walk just as Jesus walked, this is how we stay within the will of God for our lives. It is easier said than done. When we abide with God's premises we must accept or act in accordance with the "rule" of Christ. Jesus is the way, the truth and the life. That is the rule. Within that rule of following Christ – by allowing him to abide within us – we have scriptural examples of service, love, child-rearing, chastity, fidelity, fairness, prayer, and self-control.

Within the realm of the rule, it is okay to have things or important relationships with people, but what did you do to get those things or that relationship? What do you do to keep it? How are you using it or them? Are you willing to "sin" to amass, acquire, control or maintain those things or that relationship in your life?

Keep in mind that worldly things aren't just material comforts and may also present in any of the following ways:

Emotional Comfort – Do you seek out praise and admiration? Do you do things just to be seen or so that you can receive praise? Are you conceited, vain or self-seeking in your actions?

Physical Comfort – Where are you living? What did you do to get there and stay? Are you connected to a "sinful" job that pays well but you know in your heart that the work is wrong, the atmosphere is wrong, the people are wrong and you do nothing to represent God?

Sexual Comfort – Have you turned your body over to sin? Are you lustful in your daily walk? Are you dressing and grooming for attention? Ladies, could it be that the clothes you wear, the hairstyle, fingernails, and perfume you use to call attention to yourself, has dimmed the light that God put inside of you; or because of your outward cloaking, the light cannot get out? Are your heels a little higher, your skirt a little shorter and your hips swaying a little harder than normal? Guys, are you driving a car you cannot afford to boost your self-esteem and ego so that you can attract more females? Are you being less than honest with women so that they will give you what you want: time; attention; ego stroking; arm candy; babies without the responsibility of marriage; home cooked meals; gifts; access to sex; clean laundry? Simple things, necessary things, that can be sinful if the motivation is wrong.

Our foolish pride comes from this world, and so do our selfish desires and our desire to have "everything" we see. None of this comes from the Father. 1 John 2:16 (CEV) (emphasis supplied). Proverbs 16:2 reminds us that *All a person's ways seem pure to them, but motives are weighed by the Lord.* (NIV). As we go through our life's walk, we must try not to use the Word of God as a crutch that supports our bad behavior. In some instances, we allow ourselves to rest on the fact that "God knows my heart," and this is true, but in the sense of what motivates a person to seek out worldly things, God knows the issues of our heart, as well. If we are self-focused and apply our talents and gifts only to amass worldly possessions and control the people around us, God will take our motives into consideration.

Consider the story of Cain and Abel.
2. Now Abel kept flocks, and Cain worked the soil. 3. In the course of time Cain brought some of the fruits of the soil as an offering to the LORD. 4. And Abel also brought an offering—fat portions from some of the firstborn of his flock. The LORD looked with favor on Abel and his offering, 5. but on Cain and his offering he did not look with favor. So Cain was very angry, and his face was downcast. Genesis 4:2-5 (NIV).

There is nothing in this passage that alerts us to the differences in the offerings, other than the fact that God reviewed and accepted Abel's offering in accordance with what he knew about Abel's heart; and He did not accept Cain's offering in accordance with what he knew about Cain's heart. We know that God spoke to Cain and advised him that if he did "what is right," his offering would be accepted as well. Genesis 4:7.

God decides what is right or wrong with the motivation of our heart, and our ways are not His ways. Isaiah 55:8. So when you say, "God knows my heart," assume he really does, and He will know more about your heart than you know about your heart. We have to be cognizant of where we are in the process so that we can use our gifts and talents with the right motivation, to the glory of God, and the betterment of ourselves.

WHERE'S MY MOTIVATION

To initiate a successful walk with God, we must see ourselves as an actor within God's grand scheme and plan. Whether we believe we signed up for it or not, we are all actors on God's world stage. An actor is incapable of putting forth his or her best performance if he is unaware of where the writer was coming from at the time of the writing, as well as where the director wants to take the scene. In the beginning was the Word – accordingly, God is both the writer and the director – the author and the finisher of our lives.

If you have ever seen a script or even acted in an elementary school play, you know that there are directions that tell the actor which emotion is the focal point of the scene. In our daily lives with God, we can access the same process because we have the script – the Bible; and we have the director – Jesus' perfect example as he walked the earth; and the actions of the prophets for how were are to live our lives.

1. Since we have such a huge crowd of men of faith watching us from the grandstands, let us strip off anything that slows us down or holds us back, and especially those sins that wrap themselves so tightly around our feet and trip us up; and let us run with patience the particular race that God has set before us. 2. Keep your eyes on Jesus, our leader and instructor. He was willing to die a shameful death on the cross because of the joy he knew would be his afterwards; and now he sits in the place of honor by the throne of God. 3. If you want to keep from becoming fainthearted and weary, think about his patience as sinful men did such terrible things to him. 4. After all, you have never yet struggled against sin and temptation until you sweat great drops of blood. Hebrews 12:1-4 (The Living Bible).

In order to make our demons submit to the Word of God, we must first learn what motivates our demons. Which emotions trip and then trick us into believing we need worldly adulation in order to feel that we have run a successful race? If we can capture the emotions that are represented in our worldly desires then we will have an opportunity to make our personal demons submit to the name of Jesus.

How do we manage our emotions? We manage our emotions by faith, which is increased by learning the Word of God and seeking to have a true relationship with Him. In the beginning of your learning process, it may be difficult to first know the Word, and then *believe* in its manifestation such that it builds your faith that what God says is true. In the beginning of your learning to have a full relationship with God, you may only be able to utter the name Jesus. But I can tell you from experience, that there is true POWER in simply speaking his name over and over again! Believers can rest in the promise, *[a]nd these signs will accompany those who believe: In my name they will drive out demons; they will speak in new tongues; ...* Mark 16:17 (NIV).

Although we believe in all things spiritual, there is a practical application in calling out the name of Jesus. Once during a particularly tumultuous argument with my ex-spouse, I was overwhelmed by how no matter how quiet I became or how many times I tried to walk away from the confrontation, the devil continued to make mischief by having my ex follow me from room to room saying nasty things to me. At a moment when I was losing all self-control and ready to lash out at him physically, the thought came to me to drop to my knees and call out to the Lord. I stayed on the floor and repeated, "Jesus, Jesus, Jesus" over and over as loud as I could until finally, the devil gave up, and so did my ex.

No one wants to tangle with God. If you get your heart motivated in the right direction and you get your understanding of God's word, you can use your faith to your advantage as both a shield and a sword, and your devil-inspired vices will submit to the power in His name! *16. In addition to all this, take up the shield of faith, with which you can extinguish all the flaming arrows of the evil one. 17. Take the helmet of salvation and the sword of the Spirit, which is the word of God.* Ephesians 6:16-17 (NIV).

I know there are some people who are adverse to recognizing Jesus as the intercessor of our faith. In some cases the problem lies in the acceptance and explanation of the trinity, and in others, people just feel that they should be "able" to speak with God on their own. At the risk of going off topic and addressing something I may not be educated enough to argue effectively, I will simply give you some back story into my spiritual journey to Jesus.

I was not baptized or christened as a baby, but I taught myself the Lord's Prayer and the Apostle's Creed from a prayer book in my Parent's medicine cabinet when I was 6 or 7 years old. I'm not sure why I "picked" those two, other than a calling on my spirit that my conscious self knew nothing about. I visited many different churches with my friends, and at the age of 12, I was baptized AME at my Aunt's church. I enjoyed singing hymns. I listened to the sermons, but I received no religious instruction, and I was confused about who Jesus was in relation to God and the Holy Spirit. I never asked for an explanation because everyone around me seemed to already "get it." I sat quietly absorbing as much as I could about Christ.

After my first marriage dissolved, at 22 years-old, I took my Shahada and became a practicing Muslim. And when I say practicing, I mean face-to-toe-covered-Ramadan-fasting-five-times-a-day-praying-practicing-Muslim. Not only did I love the discipline, but I was smart enough to realize that I needed it to survive being a single mother of two, with no degree, no job and living in an apartment that was leased under the name of my former mother-in-law. Not a good look. I loved the peace and the power I felt every time I stepped onto my prayer rug – and I still pray on it to this day. Communing through prayer with God first thing in the morning – at sunrise (Fajr Prayer) was my favorite. And while I no longer have a name for it, praying first thing in the morning is still my favorite time to get right with God.

Many things transpired for me to come out of the practice, and most were my "fault." Like many people, as my life improved, I subconsciously felt like I needed God less and less, and the discipline became an impediment. I didn't perceive myself as a "good Muslim woman." I had too much mouth, was too opinionated and submission to a man was per se out of the question. I lacked understanding, but I respected the religion enough to not want it misrepresented. Perceiving it to be "easier," I went back to being a Christian.

Returning to Christianity created many theological issues for me. All those Trinity questions had been answered from a Muslim perspective, and now I knew that I would never be able to pray to Jesus, even if he was considered a major prophet in Islam. Only God garnered the respect of praise and worship. Despite my Muslim perspective, I managed to enjoy my church experience – it was something that I knew – and I've never shied away from any religious experience that made my spirit feel a sense of comfort. I was good with it all until it came time to say "Thank you, Jesus." That, I could not manage to do, and I always felt frozen and awkward, even though I'm sure no one recognized my spiritual angst but me.

Initially, I just didn't *want* to say it. But eventually, the time did come when I wanted to say it, and *couldn't*. At that particular time, I was really overcome by the Holy Spirit: the Pastor had preached fire; the music was playing, but I could no longer hear it. It was as if I was watching myself from a different place. My hands were raised – and that in and of itself was a stretch – and my mind was thinking, "Thank you, Jesus," but it seemed as if my lips were wired shut. Back then I didn't know how much power there was in saying that name. And now I know that it was the devil that kept me silenced, knowing how powerful I would become the moment I was able to release my spirit, confusion, and inhibitions into an atmosphere filled with God's presence. The devil wants us to be silent because he knows that at name of Jesus, our demons must submit.

What is the win of this situation, based upon what you may believe about the Trinity in general, and Jesus as an intercessor, in particular? The mere fact that you picked up this book and have gotten this far means you have determined that whatever you had been doing to take your life back needs to be enhanced in some way. I am faithful that this will happen for you as God assists my pen. It also means that wherever you are in your secular application – be it journaling, counseling (private-paid or friendship-free), or less desirable things like eating, drinking, drugs, or sexual encounters – has not been enough to get you where God needs for you to be in your purposeful life. Allow me to offer the name of Jesus to call your demons into submission, and out of your life. There IS POWER in the name of Jesus! Just say it, and take your life back!

4 WAVE THE RED FLAG

God works ... in mysterious ways. People turn to this premise when they believe that what has transpired can only be explained by the inner workings of God. And yes, in some cases I feel the same way. There are things that even if explained by science continue to be a mystery of God's power, like the creation of life, and how your body works in such an interactive way. But I've found that other things are far less mysterious when, in retrospect, I realize that I just missed God's first ten signals, and it took a mysterious coming together of events to get me to see what God said at the outset.

Red flags are real! Have you ever been in relationship with someone and witnessed a weird act of behavior that touches your insides to a quiver – a feeling that you know isn't related to love? You recognize the giant red flag waving in your face, but choose to turn the other way? I submit to you that the waver of the red flag is God. Whether you are on your knees praying for answers, or simply operating in God's grace, He is always on the case giving you what you need. We (particularly me) are simply turning a blinds eye to what God is showing us for our own good.

We make excuses because we get offered what we think is best for us at the time: He may come with a little swag, a good reputation and some money in his pockets. She may show up with a bangin' body, pretty toes, intelligent conversation, and talent in the kitchen! It may come with six-figures (or five pretty good ones), a corner office with a window view and season tickets to (insert your favorite team here)! But somewhere before we took a leap of fate, God swung the red flag, and we chose to ignore it. We meandered into a lion's den, and then questioned how we got into it, and why God would allow us to stay. All the while, where and how we find ourselves is of our own doing, because we didn't pay attention to the voice that was God inside of us.

Once entrenched, things may start to fall apart – people get revealed for the truth of who they are, and job expectations never discussed or agreed upon become the focal point of your everyday life. As God peels back the layers, and your eyes start to focus, and too many coincidences fall into place, we murmur to ourselves how God's plan is so mysterious. When in fact there was no mystery, we just MISSED it, and the unraveling is God giving us yet another chance to see things clearly in one fell swoop. And as these things start to unravel, we look back and say, I should have changed direction when this happened, or this, or this ...

And that is why we must get in tuned with our God-center, and build our relationship with God, so that the first time we see that tiny issue that quivers our stomach, we will trust our faith that God is speaking, rather than toy with fate and move forward anyway. It takes a lot of will to say NO to something that appears to be so good. But we should learn that looks and words, are often deceiving;

that the person or job that wants to use our talent, stays ready and willing to tell us what we want to hear, to get us where they need us to be. There's nothing wrong with that per se. Most of us come with a big enough ego that we believe in the goodness of self and what the other person tells us about ourselves. However, if the purpose is one of manipulation, then we can't know this at the outset, because it will be offered and presented on the best platter with full trimmings. That is why we MUST listen to God inside of us when words give us pause, or an action causes us concern. Pray on it, and ask for the strength to move away from what may eventually present itself as insufficient to meet our needs.

"For I know the plans I have for you," declares the Lord, *"plans to prosper you and not to harm you, plans to give you hope and a future."* Jeremiah 29:11 (NIV) This scripture always comes to mind when I am second-guessing that voice inside of me. It is so important to have enough confidence in yourself to allow God to lead you; to trust in Him enough to give up the things that may appear to make perfect sense to you, or things and people who bring you pseudo-comfort along with actual pain.

Don't miss God's light tap on the shoulder as a trade for the mysterious ways He can work it out at the end. He will get you out of a situation that is not prosperous for you, but you should opt for sooner rather than later. Doing so requires us to key into His power, and trust Him with all we have. Doing so requires that we pay attention when God is waving the red flag in front of our desires – even when it appears that what we have is good. Proverbs 3:5-6 reminds us to 5. *Trust in the Lord with all your heart and lean not on your own understanding; 6 in all your ways submit to him, and he will make your paths straight.* (NIV) God will paint the town red. Watch Him and take your life back!

5 USE YOUR GIFTS

SCRIPTURE 3: Every good and perfect gift is from above, coming down from the Father of the heavenly lights, who does not change like shifting shadows. James 1:17(NIV)

What gift did God give you that makes you happy to perform? It could be a specific talent like singing, dancing, or mine, which is writing. It could also be something more work related like the ability to be a surgeon, a counselor or even a pastor. It could be something more subtle, like a compassion for the poor, caring for children or ministering to the sick. Whatever your gift, there are three things that you need to remember: (1) It comes from God; (2) It is good and perfect; and (3) Its application will provide direction in your life that can manifest itself in a way that gives you control over your circumstances. Believe it or not, by using your gift, you can take your life back!

When our lives feel out of control, it is important to take inventory of anything and everything that we believe we can do well. By doing this we allow ourselves the opportunity to recognize the good within us, and how that good can be used to help others. When we use our gifts and talents to improve another person's circumstances, we take the focus off what we may feel we lack.

When we find ourselves at a low point in our lives, and possibly without direction, it is important that we tap into our talents so that we can see a little more clearly God's purpose for our life. Many of us use countless hours doing things that bring limited joy – furthering our disappointments – by failing to figure out why we were placed on this planet. I can assure you, our purpose is not just to work and pay bills.

The Bible says that before we were fashioned in our mother's womb God knew us. The Bible also tells us that in knowing us, God also had a plan for us: *"plans to prosper you and not to harm you, plans to give you hope and a future."* Jeremiah 29:11. (NIV). What the Bible does not tell us is *what* we were purposed to do. Taking stock of our gifts – what God gave us to use – is both a way we say, "Thank you," to God; and how we can find our purpose in life.

I love how the scripture in James states that "every" good and perfect gift is from God. There is no question in that scripture. Every gift is included. But how do we know we are operating in our gift? By definition, a gift is something willingly given to someone without payment; or a natural ability or talent. What a blessing that what God gives us to work our purpose in life may encompass both of those definitions.

A gift is something that you choose to use. In terms of allowing your gifts to focus your life back to order, we may consider several things once we learn exactly what our gifts might be: (1) if we focus on appreciating our gifts, we have a reference point for being grateful; (2) if we find a way to use our gifts to assist others, we feel accomplished, gain confidence; and (3) the confidence gained is the catalyst for taking our life back.

Of course, the ultimate gift that God gave to us was salvation through the sacrifice of His son, Jesus Christ. The Bible tells us in Ephesians 2:8-10 *8. For it is by grace you have been saved, through faith – and this is not from yourselves, it is the gift of God – 9. not by works, so that no one can boast. 10. For we are God's handiwork, created in Christ Jesus to do good works, which God prepared in advance for us to do.* (NIV) Therefore, our salvation is a gift – there is nothing we must do to gain it other than have faith and 9. *If you declare with your mouth, "Jesus is Lord," and believe in your heart that God raised him from the dead, you will be saved. 10. For it is with your heart that you believe and are justified, and it is with your mouth that you profess your faith and are saved.* Romans 10:9-10. (NIV). So, if we are saved by grace, and it is received as a gift, the works that we do are manifest simply in the fact that we believe in Christ, and desire to emulate his behavior. Faith without works is dead, but it is our faith that pushes us to do good works. Faith and good works combine to create a cycle – a circle that turns upon itself, and it may be fueled by using the gifts and talents with which we were born.

Finding and using our gifts for ourselves is a way that we take our lives back, and I bet you've done this unknowingly many times before. When I was a little girl and feeling out of sorts with myself or my environment, it always made me feel better to write and play with my dolls – and since I now have seven children, we apparently know how one gift worked out! As to the other, I began writing poetry and stories when I was around nine years old. I can't even imagine how elementary my scribbles must have been, but I know for sure that getting my feelings down on paper made me feel better, even if the feelings I chose to express were not "good" feelings.

When I was close to eleven, my sister bought me a diary with a lock, and it was all I could do to hold myself steady in school anticipating what I would disclose on those pages. It balanced me and gave me the opportunity to start my life again fresh each time. Once I wrote down what "needed" to be said, I felt better. But similarly, as a gift, writing brings me comfort – and when it comes out to my liking, I can reflect and enjoy it repeatedly. Not only can I enjoy it for myself, but in the times when I have been fearless, I have shared it with others to express my feelings toward them. I write poems about people and my heart.

What about music? How many times have you felt down and put on your favorite tune – or even better – used your own vocal talent to sing yourself into a state of calm? There is something about the sound of music that changes the nature of the room. David directs us in Psalm 95:2, *Let us come before him with thanksgiving and extol him with music and song.* (NIV) The need for music – to receive it and to offer it – is within us. God does not give us a task that we cannot handle – so we all are capable of singing praises to the Lord with our self-assigned harmony. Some tunes may sound better than others, but we can clap our hands, or stomp our feet, or raise our voices. The praise is the "song" that brings us into the presence of God in our own lives! *Enter his gates with thanksgiving and his courts with praise; give thanks to him and praise his name.* Psalm 100:4 (NIV). Take your life back.

In times when I have been through some of my worst relationship issues, I have turned to music to soothe and calm my spirit. Many times, I would simply put in my ear-buds, place the iPod on shuffle, and let it play until I fell asleep. Sometimes, I sang to myself, and sometimes I sang out loud. Sometimes I was silent and let the tears fall to my pillow. But I always felt better. It is perhaps innate, to understand how music soothes you, but it is divine confirmation to learn that it also soothed King Saul in the Bible. *And it came to pass, when the evil spirit from God was upon Saul, David took an harp, and played with his hand: so Saul was refreshed, and was well, and the evil spirit departed from him.* 1 Samuel 16:23 (KJV).

As you can see, it doesn't have to be your gift for it to be good and perfect. Because my gift is writing, I find a great sense of peace in reading. When I am in a funk, walking into a bookstore is very much like walking into the sanctuary for me. Truly, I feel the presence of God when I am surrounded by books. The smell of the newness, the feel of the pages, the emotions the words make me feel, are all a part of recognizing my personal and perfect gift from God. Honing your gift is another way to say, "Thank you" to God. For me, writing, reading and being in the presence of words, are part and parcel, and cannot be separated.

Honing your gift also prepares you for the next level when your gift will be used to God's glory. When you find and focus your time on your talent, you realize you are doing something that you love, and you are inherently good in that action. This is a self-esteem booster. Anything that boosts your self-esteem raises your confidence level. Confidence replaces fear. When you are no longer afraid, you can make decisions about your life that will bring you the greatest benefit. Finding your talent, honing your skill, and sharing your gift, will allow you to walk with a purpose and take your life back.

A very important part of taking your life back is to honor God with your gifts. You do this simply by using the potential they bring. Making a conscious effort to use our gifts prevents us from paying too much attention to what or who helped us veer from our original path, or keeps us from our most righteous path. There is goodness and mercy on the path of righteousness, and it will follow you all the days of your life. (Psalm 23)

Not only did God give us the gifts that we find most familiar – the creative ones – He also gave us spiritual gifts that manifest out of our relationship with Him and the Word. Our spiritual gifts are not likely ones that you would think of outright. In Romans 12:6-8, we are told that we all have spiritual gifts that we must use:

6. We have different gifts, according to the grace given to each of us. If your gift is prophesying, then prophesy in accordance with your faith; 7. if it is serving, then serve; if it is teaching, then teach; 8. if it is to encourage, then give encouragement; if it is giving, then give generously; if it is to lead, do it diligently; if it is to show mercy, do it cheerfully. (NIV)

In 1 Corinthians 12:8-10, we find some of the same gifts and then a few more given to us by the Holy Spirit:

To one there is given through the Spirit a message of wisdom, to another a message of knowledge by means of the same Spirit, 9.to another faith by the same Spirit, to another gifts of healing by that one Spirit, 10. to another miraculous powers, to another prophecy, to another distinguishing between spirits, to another speaking in different kinds of tongues, and to still another the interpretation of tongues. (NIV).

How glorious it is to know that God placed something inside of all of us, that if we take the time to build our relationship with Him, we may be able to assist others in finding their way to Christ. When you begin to take your life back by focusing on your spiritual growth and development of your God-consciousness, you will find that your spiritual gifts will start to appear to you. As you learn the Word and become more familiar with its passages, you will find that you have an ability to perform one or more of the spiritual gifts identified above.

I remember when I first started going to Bible study. At the end of the class, the Pastor would have us separate into small groups for prayer. I never liked being in the small groups even though I knew that community prayer – touching and agreeing with another – would ensure that God would be in our midst. I needed the community because I wasn't that great at feeling the presence of God, but I was afraid to tell what I needed, and even more afraid that I would be placed in a group where I would be asked to lead the prayer. I knew I was not a prayer warrior. I could not put my words together in cadenced speech with perfectly-pitched rises, and a recall of the scripture that would make anyone feel like I had convened with God on his or her behalf. I typically tried to find a group where I knew there would be someone with that gift who would be eager to "pray us up." However fearful I was to lead, I learned that as I focused on my own spiritual growth, without my own knowledge, I *became* a prayer warrior.

On the first night when I found myself in a group of "newbies," no one wanted to pray. I certainly didn't want to do it, but the room had already grown loud with the murmurs from ten separate groups, and I didn't want our group to fall behind. I opened my mouth and out came words from God. I prayed for everyone and everything. I remembered every request; I had scripture to back up the need; and even though my armpits were sweating profusely and my speech was probably a little labored, I made it through and the people in my group felt relieved that someone had interceded on their behalf. God will always make sure that you are ready when He needs you to be ready, but you must take the time to be prepared so that God knows that you want to help build the Kingdom.

This preparation – learning and using your gifts – will help you take your life back. Do not leave this world full of your potential, so that when God pulls up the big screen and reviews your life He turns to you and says, "Great, you accomplished this – but, if you had utilized your talents as I intended, *this* is where I wanted you to be!"

Writing this book is my attempt to use my talents and not depart spiritually from this earth without maximizing God's purpose for my life. In my own mind, I see myself as a New York Times bestselling author, ten times over. If this is what I envision for myself, trying to reach my own goals should lead me to God's ultimate goal for my life and His glory. I may have deviations along the way, but if I stay the course of my talents – accepting any additions that present as I grow in my gifts – I will align myself with God, and be on my way to fulfilling my destiny. You will, too. With a destiny-filled, purpose-driven life, you will place your life under God's control and out of the hands of the enemy. Use your gifts and take life back!

6 BUT MY GIFTS ARE FEELING USED

Last night when I went to bed, I felt overwhelmed and under-appreciated—I say under because people always give me a little somethin' somethin' to keep me going, but from time to time, I allow the issues of the day to consume me to a point of defeat. I should never let that happen. The nature of feeling this way comes not from any inadequacy from within, but from taking on what I perceive are another person's value judgments about my level of performance. When you know you are trying your best, but for one reason or another it is not shining through to the people around you, you may feel defeated. You shouldn't.

Everyone has a level of ability that God gave to them before they were created in the womb. *"Before I formed you in the womb I knew you, before you were born I set you apart; I appointed you as a prophet to the nations."* Jeremiah 1:5 (NIV) Okay, so maybe we're not all going to be the one called to guide nations, but on a smaller scale, whatever your role is within your family, your church, your profession, etc. is what you have been called to do in the moment.

Let's look at it from this perspective: your talents were already there, but whatever they are, you had to nurture them in some way. Even a gifted musician who can play by ear won't get any better if she doesn't listen and practice her craft. Sometimes our gifts are obvious, but other times, we take on jobs that may not come naturally for us. If we are trying our best and nothing is flowing smoothly, we might tend to want to give up. Right? Of course, that is natural.

In the Garden of Gethsemane, it's safe to say that based upon the scripture, Jesus was overwhelmed, and likely feeling under-appreciated. Although I surely can't put words in his mouth, Jesus said, *"My soul is overwhelmed with sorrow to the point of death. Stay here and keep watch with me."* Matthew 26:38. (NIV) Surrounded by the people he'd chosen to accompany him, Jesus found himself with little assistance when all he asked was for them to stay awake—a simple request. In real time, putting myself in Jesus' position for a moment, I'm thinking: with all that I've shown you, shared with you and given you, you can't even do one little thing? Whatever that one little thing might be, if it isn't performed, I'm feeling some kind of way: (1) overwhelmed – because I asked for your help; and (2) unappreciated – because you didn't "care" enough to help me; and (3) used – because if I don't do it, no one else will do it. Okay, out of Jesus mode.

Jesus went away and prayed, *"My Father, if it is not possible for this cup to be taken away unless I drink it, may your will be done."* Matthew 26:42. (NIV) We all know how the story ends: Jesus gives the ultimate sacrifice because there was no one else to do it. He certainly wasn't appreciated for it at the time. And by some who are outside of the realm of belief, he still remains unappreciated.

My brother once shared a discussion he had with his

pastor who informed, 'if the people didn't appreciate Jesus, what makes you think someone is going to appreciate you?' I try to come back to this nugget of information when I'm allowing others to affect my joy. Appreciation for Jesus' sacrifice was not to be had in the moment, but he did it anyway for the greater good, knowing that what he was about to accomplish no one else could do but him.

I am not suggesting you be a martyr. However, it would help you to understand that everyone has a calling and a purpose, and whatever role you play in your family, church, or profession is yours to do at 100%. Not for recognition or praise, not even to be appreciated, but only so that God will be glorified in the work that you did, and hopefully in the outcome of the person who benefits. Allow your gifts to be used in love.

7 HOW DO YOU HEAR GOD?

To move forward you must know how you hear God when He speaks to you. You must be aware of your system of communication – when and how God speaks to you – so that you know you are hearing clearly and correctly.

God speaks to me mainly through His Word – the Holy Bible. Actually, I have had many instances where I have opened the Bible to what I believed was a random passage, only to find that the chapter and verse most notable on the page provided specific direction in my life. It was through a random opening of the Bible that I realized that God does speak, and He does it in such a manner that you will be responsive, because you know that only God could know you that well.

God admonished me right before I started writing Chapter 9 of this book. At one point in my spiritual journey, when life was very difficult, I was an avid prayer warrior, student of the Bible and meditation. In the morning I carved out an hour so that I could pray, read scripture and study before I went to work. On Sunday I went to my local church at 7:30 AM, then came home to watch my current local church (Redemption) on-line at 10:30AM. (Nerd Alert) At the end of the night, I would watch sermon replays of T.D. Jakes and Pastor Touré Robert's and take notes. On Tuesday nights I had Bible study; on Wednesday night I had Women's Ministry; on Thursday night I had on-line Life Groups; and on Saturday my prayer and mediation sessions could last for two hours or more. I constantly read workbooks and spiritual articles and took many trips to the bookstore just to see what God had for me sitting on the shelves. (That's another way he speaks to me, but in the interest of time I will skip it).

Back in 2014, I did nothing for my spiritual growth. Discouraged with my lack of progress, I challenged myself to attend all fifty-two weeks of services for 2015, which I did. But after I received word from God that I could move to Greenville, South Carolina to increase my spiritual knowledge and social/service connections, my commitment once again diminished. Yes, I still went to church – every week – and I still read and listened to some choice sermons, but my Bible reading and study, and even more so, my prayer and meditation became less and less, the more joy I felt in my life. The problem with this, other than the obvious, is that the more in tune you are with your spirit, the more God will reveal Himself to you and the plans He has for you.

Right before I left for Greenville is when I received the revelation of this book. For seven mornings straight I woke up with a particular scripture on my mind. When the seventh scripture was given to me, the next night I received the premise of this book and the purpose for the revelation of scripture. Until this was revealed to me, I believed that the scriptures were given to me to protect me from the negative behavior between me and my spouse at the time. Each day I woke up and wrote down the scripture with colored markers on a yellow legal pad. After writing them out, I pinned them to my pillows so that if he ventured into my room while I was at work, he would be confronted, and hopefully convicted, by the Word of God.

I started the book while still living in Florida, but much like my prayer, meditation and study, I began to procrastinate and slack off out of a little joy, but mostly fear. When I had muddled through three of seven scriptures I was utterly paralyzed at the thought of addressing the next chapter in my own words and application. Each time I attempted to write something I became filled with the fear of failure and then became physically ill to the point that I could not write even if I wanted.

It was a very interesting predicament because I knew all along that crafting this book would be the beginning of my destiny. I should have been excited and well prepared. I felt neither, only fear, and loathing the process. But as I noticed my life becoming stagnate, I made a conscious effort to try, or at least try about trying. On that day, I went to my car during my break-time at work, and taking my Bible with me, I was going to read over my notes so that I could begin. But once again, when I opened my Bible to a "random" page, I found myself in the Book of Revelation – the only Book I had purposely not read. This is what I received:

1. "To the angel of the church in Ephesus write: These are the words of him who holds the seven stars in his right hand and walks among the seven golden lampstands. 2. I know your deeds, your hard work and your perseverance. I know that you cannot tolerate wicked people, that you have tested those who claim to be apostles but are not, and have found them false. 3. You have persevered and have endured hardships for my name, and have not grown weary. 4. Yet I hold this against you: You have forsaken the love you had at first. 5 Consider how far you have fallen! Repent and do the things you did at first. If you do not repent, I will come to you and remove your lampstand from its place. The Book of Revelation 2:1-5 (NIV)

This passage was significant for many reasons: First, it directly addressed my failure to pray, meditate and study like I had done prior to moving to Greenville. Truly, I had fallen from my first love when I couldn't get enough. Second, the scripture spoke directly to my fear and procrastination regarding an upcoming chapter of this book. More pointedly, that chapter was specifically about Zerubbabel and the seven lampstands. The revelation confirmed my belief that this book was the beginning of my Godly purpose and destiny, and if I failed to write it, my lampstand (my gift and ability to move to my next level) would be taken away. So, with a renewed sense of purpose, and a mutation of my fear of failure into fear of losing my gift, I began writing of how Zechariah Chapter 4 can help you take your life back with confidence.

God speaks in many ways. It is imperative that you learn your language and listen to hear it. It was only because I had enough encounters with God that the Chapter in Revelation presented itself to me with such significance. Your best life depends on how you communicate with God and He back to you. Listen carefully and take your life back!

.

8 STICK AND MOVE

Journal Entry: This morning I lay in bed too long, and now I'm late. One of the reasons is because I just couldn't figure out anything to write that was worth writing. No, that's not actually true, I have an idea for what needs to be written, but I've been putting it off. – it's that piece on Unconditional Love. I guess since God gave it to me a week ago, and I haven't moved on it, things might be a little more difficult until I get to His business. But work with me God, I'm trying to go in another direction…

Therein stems the problem.

When I was younger, I used to wonder why God never talked to me; why he never seemed to answer my prayers when I spoke with Him. My aunt was a great prayer warrior, and I could *see* her belief – that in her spirit, she really did converse with God on a regular basis, and He conversed back. So, when she told me to pray on it— whatever juvenile thing it was at the moment—it never crossed my mind that there was something more that I needed to do: *listen* for an answer. I just assumed I wasn't special enough to get an answer. I found out many years later that we are all worthy of an answer, even if the answer is no.

What I found out about myself, and maybe you have learned this as well, is that you must stick around in God's presence long enough to listen for the answer, and then *move in that direction.* The key is trusting God enough to make the move if the answer is not what you anticipated.

I learned this premise from a guest pastor when I lived in Tallahassee. His ultimate message was to ask God to give you *sight beyond sight,* and that once you asked those key questions in your life through prayer, you had to listen. On the drive home from that sermon, I turned to my former husband and asked: "If you asked God to give you sight beyond sight, and prayed for Him to show you who was good for you, and who was not, and He said I was completely on the 'kick that one to the curb' list, would you listen and do it?" Now, of course, I followed this up with an "it's okay to be honest, I won't get mad…," and he answered confidently with a "no."

Given that we were in turmoil at the time, my question may have been tongue in cheek or just somewhat devilish – hoping that if he answered, "Yes," it might have given me a little more leeway to exit sooner rather than later. That did not happen; however, it did bring to light how committed we must be to God if we really want to find ourselves where God has us purposed. It won't always be easy. Once you ask God for an answer, and He gives it to you, if you don't react on it the way you have been instructed, your path to His purpose for you is likely to be much longer, and heavy with unnecessary burdens. Knowing this may not make the decision-making process any easier. However, we must be spiritually mature in making our choices. Strength is required!

In the past, my inability to hear God was more so

based on my not wanting to hear that answer. I heard the tiny voice, felt that movement, had that dream. I knew what it was on some level, but it didn't fit into what I wanted at the time, so I ignored it, and opted to go in another direction. I've suffered many deviations because of my inability to stick around long enough to receive God's answer, and then move in God's direction. I have learned by trial, and many errors, to listen and then trust the answer God gives me in whatever medium He selects at the time.

Stay in His presence. Listen. Move in His direction. Take your life back!

9 KEEP THE FIRE BURNING

SCRIPTURE 4: What are you, O great mountain? Before Zerubbabel you will become a plain; and he will bring forth the top stone with shouts of "Grace, grace to it!" Zechariah 4:7 (New American Standard Bible)

When our lives are off kilter and out of control, we see in great detail every obstacle and mountain we have to climb. Getting ourselves fixated on the problem does not help us make the problem go away. Focusing on the pile of bills, the mountains of homework, numerous projects at work, relationships that are out of balance, and anything else that seems insurmountable, keeps our lives in a state of flux. We remain frazzled, sometimes being completely unable to concentrate long enough, even to make our prayers and petitions sound remotely plausible to ourselves. And yes, the Holy Spirit hears our groans, and takes our petitions to God, but sometimes *we* need a tangible reminder that we are in fact "speaking to our mountains."

In Mark 11:23, Jesus explained, *"Truly I tell you, if anyone says to this mountain, 'Go, throw yourself into the sea,' and does not doubt in their heart but believes that what they say will happen, it will be done for them.* (NIV) But how do we manifest this scripture? I submit that your mountains are thrown into the sea when you align yourself with God's will and purpose for your life. Alignment allows you to get your anointing. Operating in your anointing is your best assurance that you are in the will of God. But how do you find your alignment to get your anointing, to apply your talent, and then level those mountains and take your life back? As a reminder from Chapter 5, find your talent, work your talent and minister to the people who come into your presence.

Is your life aligned with God's plan for you? In order for you to maximize your blessings, you must be in alignment with God's intention for you. When you are aligned with God, you give yourself full access to your anointing. To be anointed literally means to rub oil onto someone or something. It also means to confer divinity or a blessing on an action. So you can be anointed to sing, anointed to dance, anointed to preach or even to write. The Bible tells us in Zechariah that God looks for people to anoint, and that the oil for the anointing will never run out. The oil is always available, and it is found in those seven lampstands we briefly discussed in Chapter 7.

Zechariah 4:1-7, is filled with imagery and metaphors. However, even if you take the reading at face value, you will see how God intends to bless us on a continuous basis. When we stay in His presence, we have the capability to remove every mountain from our path:

Then the angel who talked with me returned and woke me up, like someone awakened from sleep. 2. He asked me, "What do you see?" I answered, "I see a solid gold lampstand with a bowl at the top and seven lamps on it, with seven channels to the lamps. 3. Also there are two olive trees by it, one on the right of the bowl and the other on its left." 4. I asked the angel who talked with me, "What are these, my lord?" 5. He answered, "Do you not know what these are?" "No, my lord," I replied. 6 So he said to me, "This is the word of the Lord to Zerubbabel: 'Not by might nor by power, but by my Spirit,' says the Lord Almighty. 7 "What are you, mighty mountain? Before Zerubbabel you will become level ground. Then he will bring out the capstone to shouts of 'God bless it! God bless it! [Grace! Grace to it (NASB)]"' Zechariah 4:1-7 (NIV).

Why is this important in taking your life back?

Zerubbabel was charged with the rebuilding of the temple after it had been destroyed. Much like our own lives, there are people and circumstances that "destroy" who we once were. It can come in the form of disease or another health issue, job loss, family dysfunction, or romantic relationships gone awry. Whatever the issue, we may feel like our own sense of self, our own self-worth, confidence or finances have been destroyed. In essence, we, like Zerubbabel, must rebuild our temple – our temple being our own bodies in a mental, physical and spiritual form.

Zerubbabel's vision is filled with symbolism that is far outside of the realm of this text. It would be good as you move through this journey to study it as you mature in your walk with Christ. But you don't have to be on "Level Ten" in order to get this and take your life back.

In the vision, there are two olive trees on either side of a bowl, filling the bowl with its oil. The trees are firmly planted and always ripe. They continuously fill the bowl, and the bowl never lacks enough oil to keep the seven lampstands lit.

How does this apply to our lives?

The bowl is your anointing from God – the supply you were given at birth. The scriptures reveal that God searches the earth back and forth, looking for someone to bless with an anointing (oil) that will never run out. *(The seven lamps represent the eyes of the LORD that search all around the world.)*. Once you are firmly planted in the Word and aligned with God's purpose for you, you have full access to the anointing. Chronicles 16:9; Zechariah 4:10.

God does not start anything in you that he doesn't intend to finish. Regardless of the mountain facing you, God's anointing gives you the power to take your life back and complete what the flesh sees as impossible. Zerubbabel was aligned with God such that he could address the rebuilding of the temple ruins, which on a natural or secular level appeared to be insurmountable; but with his alignment and the assistance of the Holy Spirit, God affirmed through Zechariah that what was started with Zerubbabel's hands would be finished by Zerubbabel's hands. Zechariah 4:9.

In order to rebuild your temple and take your life back, you will need to find your gift and start small. Consider the project you started that remains unfinished in the physical and in your heart. Begin anew and work it completely in accordance to God's purpose for you. *"... Do not despise the small beginnings, for the Lord rejoices to see the work begin, to see the plumb line in Zerubbabel's hand."* Zechariah 4:10 (NLT)

The scripture says that Zerubbabel was "plumb." Being plumb means to do something exactly or completely. It is the beginning of your reconstruction. Webster's Dictionary defines plumb in this way: a lead weight attached to a line that is used to indicate vertical direction (upright). When something is off plumb, it is out of vertical or true – out of alignment, not upright – Got it?

People often get caught up in what their purpose in life must be – I was no different – I spent countless hours reading, researching, and praying for what God wanted me to "do." What I found after all of that work is that God wants me, and you, to work our talent in accordance with the Word; be upright; start small; and stay the course to His glory. Because he continuously searches the earth with his seven eyes, He will find us and bless us while we are living out our lives as close to righteousness as we can get at that moment. With the anointed blessing of doing what we are talented to do, the mountains that were in front of us, like those before Zerubbabel, will be like plains, and rebuilding our personal temple with the assistance of the Holy Spirit will be accomplished. We must learn to embody and then shout, "Grace! Grace!" and the mountains will be leveled before us.

This is all about faith – with faith you can believe that your mountains will actually be leveled. When you are plumb – upright and level with the Word – and tied into your faith, your perspective will change, and your mountain may no longer appear to be as large as it once was before you walked the walk.

There is power in knowing what you were anointed to do. The scriptures tell us that we may not know the time when God is going to restore us completely, but you will receive power when the Holy Spirit comes on you. (Acts 1:8 NIV). In your time of prayer, confer with God and ask Him to allow the Holy Spirit to minister to your pains, and anoint your presence so that you may focus fully on the works God has set before you. Do not focus on the bills or the food or the job or the relationship or your health, *"but seek ye first the kingdom of God, and his righteousness; and all these things shall be added unto you."* Matthew 6:33 (KJV) In due time, you will take your life back. The oil is ever-present and always available to you – listen for God's whisper; and respond with a prayer; a groan; or an all-out cry.

1 Kings 19:11-12. *11. The LORD said, "Go out and stand on the mountain in the presence of the LORD, for the LORD is about to pass by." Then a great and powerful wind tore the mountains apart and shattered the rocks before the LORD, but the LORD was not in the wind. After the wind there was an earthquake, but the LORD was not in the earthquake. 12. After the earthquake came a fire, but the LORD was not in the fire. And after the fire came a gentle whisper.* (NIV).

We are reminded in Zechariah 4:6 that the victory will come, but *'Not by might nor by power, but by my Spirit,' says the Lord Almighty. (NIV)* Therefore, we must engage the Holy Spirit on our behalf:

In Prayer: 1 Corinthians 14:15 (ESV) *What am I to do? I will pray with my spirit, but I will pray with my mind also; I will sing praise with my spirit, but I will sing with my mind also.*

By our groans: Romans 8:26 (NIV) *In the same way, the Spirit helps us in our weakness. We do not know what we ought to pray for, but the Spirit himself intercedes for us through wordless groans.*

When we cry out: Psalm 37:17-18 (NIV) *17. The righteous cry out, and the LORD hears them; he delivers them from all their troubles. 18. The LORD is close to the brokenhearted and saves those who are crushed in spirit.*

Our lampstand has the potential to always be lit, as long as we stay aligned and work our talents. What we must know and understand is that however we convey our heart, the Holy Spirit is there to take our petitions to God, so that His promises can be returned to us, and our mountains may be leveled.

You *will* take your life back shouting, Grace! Grace!

10 WALK LIKE AN EGYPTIAN

You may have guessed from the chapter title that I grew up somewhere in the eighties. You can't call me an 80's baby – most likely because I started having my own kids right in the middle. In 1986, when the Bangles came out with "Walk Like an Egyptian," I was a married teenager, knowing little to nothing, and about to give birth to my first child. Thanks to the video age, we saw the group's contorted hands and feet, with facial expressions and head-movements to match, encouraging all who cared to listen to walk like an Egyptian. We all bought into it, white and black, and we had fun.

Well, what if we encouraged each other now to walk like a Christian?

Okay, so I admit, there won't be any blaring music, and you won't be adorned in poorly crafted colored outfits. But, if you are showing yourself to be full of light, much like the video, you can have people follow your lead. Why is that of any consequence? It may not be important to you unless you are power hungry and running for some political office—perhaps those are even the same things—

but, it is extra-important if you believe your purpose is to show the people around you what an AWESOME God you serve.

God's grace is a wonderful thing. It wakes you up in the morning, and gives you the ability to complain about having to get out of bed to go to the job that you hate; or tend to the kids who have been driving you crazy, even while you slept. It's God's grace that provides the leaky roof over your head, and gives you the strength to shovel all of the snow that blocks you in from getting to that job that we already know you hate. It's God's grace that gives you the breath to curse your spouse for something trivial or more. I know many people don't believe that God deals in the negative, but without the grace of that initial breath, you can't even focus on everything that is wrong in your life, and you certainly can't respond to it.

So, I challenge you (and myself) to choose instead to recognize what's going right in your life. To engage in a joyful and happy spirit despite everything else that might be going wrong right in this moment. But he said to me, *"My grace is sufficient for you, for my power is made perfect in weakness." Therefore I will boast all the more gladly about my weaknesses, so that Christ's power may rest on me.* 2 Corinthians 12:9. (NIV)

Steve Harvey encourages his listeners to, "fake it until you make it." I will give you my take on that premise in the next Chapter, but I submit to you, that if you really have your Christian light on, the joy that you feel from knowing God's grace doesn't require faking. *Whoever claims to live in him must live as Jesus did.* 1 John 2:6. (NIV) If you recognize that you are walking in God's grace then you are feeling the love. And if you're feeling the love, then the Spirit remains lifted in all circumstances. That knowledge translates into your everyday life, and you begin to appreciate your life and circumstances a little bit more.

But grow in the grace and knowledge of our Lord and Savior Jesus Christ. To him be the glory both now and forever! Amen. 2 Peter 3:18. (NIV)

In other words, walk like a Christian, and take your life back!

11 WHAT ABOUT THOSE WEAPONS?

SCRIPTURE 5: No weapon formed against you shall prosper. And every tongue which rises against you in judgment You shall condemn. This is the heritage of the servants of the Lord, And their righteousness is from Me says the Lord. Isaiah 54:17 (NKJV)

Fake it till you make it! That's what I've always thought about when I heard this scripture. "No weapon formed against you shall prosper." Really? We throw it out into the universe every chance we get, and sing it at the top of our lungs when Fred Hammond comes on the radio; but I still never embraced its potential authenticity.

To me, I thought it was a "fake" only because it is difficult to believe in the moment when daggers are stabbing you in your back, and rocks are collecting to form stumbling blocks in front of you, that your purpose is not being completely thwarted. But this is where faith comes in, in such a way that it reformulates your perspective about what is being done for you, verses what is being done to you.

The scripture is definitive and it comes with some bad news: there is a weapon and it will be formed against you! The weapon may present as a person sabotaging your efforts and attempts to get ahead at work; in your business; with your finances; or within your relationships. Sometimes the weapon may even be self-sabotage and negative speak against your own best interests out of a fear of success; a fear of failure; or a subconscious thought that you are not worthy of your next level blessings. The power of life and death is in the tongue – so we must know our own enemy so that we recognize the weapon for who or what it is.

In writing this book I have always had the concern that I did not have enough networking know-how to garner a publishing deal. My thoughts regarding self-publishing made me believe that I would never have the disposable income to publish in a manner that would make me and God proud. In this example, the weapon was two-fold: (1) Factually speaking, I did not have the contacts to move forward; and (2) My perception of my financial situation: as a single mother raising the last three of seven children; on half the salary I had been accustomed; and starting my life over from scratch in a new city without the use of my professional license, I definitely did not have the finances to move forward on my own. Those weapons formed, and they were real. So, how did I address this issue? I kept on writing by faith, hoping that when I was done, the finances (or anything else) would be made available for me – and since you are in fact reading this, you know that my faith paid off.

By believing that the obstacles in our lives will not overtake our destiny, we can regain control of our fears and doubts and take our lives back. Many of us have concerns about negative talk about us from our own conscience, co-workers, family, and friends alike. I'm not

61

just talking rumors and unsubstantiated gossip. Let's face it, some of our past actions have been less than stellar, and as my best sister-friend has always said, "Everyone has a chapter in their lives that he or she does not want read out loud."

So, what happens when there is so much internal or external chatter about you that even the walls are whispering? You cleave to Isaiah 54:17 where it states that "every tongue which rises against you in judgment you shall condemn." (NKJV).

In order to work this, you must first be aware of what it means to condemn. By condemning something, you express your complete disapproval of the words. This does not have to be an actual disapproval – although you can speak things into and out of existence as a child of God – but a spiritual one which will manifest itself with your successful completion of God's work in you. What you believe about yourself – good or bad – will never be as important as what God believes about you. You need to believe what God says about you in the Bible. He has given you the right to take your life back:

You are a child of God: *So in Christ Jesus you are all children of God through faith.* Galatians 3:26 (NIV)

You are an heir to all of God's promises: *And since we are his children, we are his heirs.* Romans 8:17 (NLT)

You are loved: *But God showed his great love for us by sending Christ to die for us while we were still sinners.* Romans 5:8 (NLT)

You are a new person: *This means that anyone who belongs to Christ has become a new person. The old life is gone; a new life has begun!* 2 Corinthians 5:17 (NLT)

You have the Holy Spirit: *And you also were included in Christ when you heard the message of truth, the gospel of your salvation. When you believed, you were marked in him with a seal, the promised Holy Spirit.* Ephesians 1:13 (NIV)

You are made to do good works: *For we are God's handiwork, created in Christ Jesus to do good works, which God prepared in advance for us to do.* Ephesians 2:10 (NIV)

You are bold and confident: *Because of Christ and our faith in him, we can now come boldly and confidently into God's presence.* Ephesians 3:12 (NLT)

With the Word of God you condemn the judgments of everyone around you and move forward with your life's work. You take your life back when you understand and believe that with God as your Father, you are protected from ultimate loss. Isaiah 54:17 clearly states that the protection of God is your heritage. Your heritage is where you originate, and it is what has been passed down to you, generation after generation. It cannot be taken from you, and you can use your position to take your life back.

Heritage is a property that descends to an heir. You should know that as a child of God, you have an inheritance in God's kingdom. As a kingdom citizen, you are born into that right and it cannot be taken from you. You possess the protections from wrong-doing prospering against you as a born child of God, and a servant to His purpose.

Please be clear that your inheritance cannot be taken away, but you must be operating at a level of maturity in order to possess it. Like any other inheritance, there are requirements that go along with the possession, whether it be as simple as age, or some other requirement written by the giver. Similarly, Isaiah 54:17 helps us to understand that we are protected from weapons prospering against us when we are "servants of the Lord." We must be operating at a level of maturity to fully invoke our God-given protection.

This is another operation of faith, when spiritual maturity may require us to act in a certain way. As God's servant, it may be very difficult to watch people, things, and circumstances attempt to force you off of your righteous path. Faith requires that we realize that there is an immediate event, and operating righteously around that event is God's ultimate plan for us. *And we know that in all things God works for the good of those who love him, who have been called according to his purpose.* Romans 8:28 (NIV).

So, now we know we can faith it until we make it! The faith operates to comfort us through the tares of life, knowing that every test we pass becomes another part of God's ultimate story for our lives. When we know that we can rely on the promise of Isaiah 54:17, we can meditate on the scripture, and apply it to the things in our lives that are beyond our control. It is the belief that nothing will undue God having the glory for the triumphs in our lives; so that whatever is thrown at us, or said about us will fail: either because it is inapplicable to our immediate situation or because we overcame the obstacle and took our lives back from the enemy. You will be free from guilt or sin and justified in your success because God made it so.

23. for all have sinned and fall short of the glory of God, 24. and all are justified freely by his grace through the redemption that came by Christ Jesus. Romans 3:23-24 (NIV)

12 TRANSFORMATION

SCRIPTURE 6: Do not conform to the pattern of this world, but be transformed by the renewing of your mind. Then you will be able to test and approve what God's will is – his good, pleasing and perfect will. Romans 12:2 (NIV)

Transformers – more than meets the eye... If you remember that cartoon, you recall that the Autobots, assisted by a father and son, transformed from one thing, to a bigger and better thing, as needed to harness energy from the earth to send back to their home. What you saw on the outside was merely a shell that embodied what was truly on the inside – that which was required to operate at the next level. Taking your life back and moving to your next God-level will require that you transform – with help from the Father and Son – into a new creature in Christ.

As human beings, we have convinced ourselves that we require certain creature comforts to be happy. For the most part, we have been conditioned since childhood to want a life that looks and feels a certain way to be content. Those of us who came from means are typically motivated to do everything in our power to keep it, increase it, and maintain that specific lifestyle. Those of us who came from a life of poverty and lack are typically motivated to try and amass a higher level of comfort than we had in the past.

We can be motivated by abundance, and we can be motivated by lack. When we are motivated by either, we are likely fixated on the things that do not increase our spiritual awareness, because our minds are focused on amassing worldly possessions and worldly positions. To take our spiritual life back from the desire for worldly gains, we must elevate the nourishment of our spirit above the comforts of our flesh.

Romans 12:2 commands: *Do not conform to the pattern of this world, but be transformed by the renewing of your mind. Then you will be able to test and approve what God's will is – his good, pleasing and perfect will.* (NIV) This scripture is a helpful start with taking back your life because it fully encompasses the other scriptures in this book. When we begin to utilize our gifts and talents for God's glory, we also begin the process of renewing our minds. Our focus shifts from gaining from the world, to giving to the world what God has placed inside of our hearts.

Transforming our minds so that we may fully invoke our hearts, is a process that requires progress. It is difficult to transform our minds when there are so many other things vying for our attention, but doing so is necessary to take your life back. In Chapter 3, we considered what some "worldly things" might be, whether material, financial, job related, or based on various relationships, and how those things can derail us. The Book of Hebrews instructs us to keep our minds focused on Jesus so that we may run the race set before us with endurance. In Philippians 4:8 we are encouraged to meditate on things that are pure, right, excellent, beautiful and positive. By focusing on the positive spiritual things, it "prevents" us from focusing solely on worldly things. The beautiful part about being able to do this is that it will subconsciously order our steps toward a righteous way of life. In that way, we don't have to be worried about what may be considered a worldly desire. If we meditate on the purity of each circumstance or situation – like finding the silver lining in every cloud – our desires will change along with our mindset.

In Psalm 37:4, David tells us to: *Take delight in the Lord, and he will give you the desires of your heart.*(NIV). This scripture has always intrigued me because I originally believed that it was straight forward: If I desire, I ask, and I get. But, as Bishop T.D. Jakes says, "the Word never addresses the obvious," and so, I also concerned myself with the question of 'what if my flesh desired something negative or something that isn't good for me' – what then? Will God give me that desire, as well? Fortunately, scriptures do not exist separate from one another, so while God will give me the desires of my heart, those desires must be in alignment with the Word for me to receive my blessing. But more importantly, if I am no longer worldly focused, but focused on what is good, pure and excellent, my mindset will change, my heart will change, and the desires of my heart will reflect the God in me. *For the mouth speaks what the heart is full of.* Luke 6:45. (NIV) The desires of my heart will be given in accordance with the God in me – one depends on the other. *Ask and it will be given to you; seek and you will find; knock and the door will be opened to you.* Matthew 7:7. (NIV)

In order to take your life back, you must not conform to what the world holds up as desirable. This is not just material, but this also includes emotional triggers that derail our forward progress. We must not seek revenge against the person we believe wronged us, or refuse to extend forgiveness to our offenders. The world will tell you that you must maintain a stoic position that dishonors a forgiving spirit, because cheek-turning is weakness, and payback should be inflicted. But that worldly belief keeps us tied to our oppressor, tied to our pasts, and our minds locked in a perpetual state of negativity.

Negative energy prevents us from meditating on the goodness of God, as Romans 12:2 suggests, because we are entirely focused on what we don't have or what someone did to us. Being tied to our negativity prevents us from being grateful for the positive things that are going on in our lives. And if you believe you are in a place where nothing is right and everything is wrong, you can simply be grateful for the sacrifice of the Risen Savior, Jesus Christ. Because of Him you have an example to focus on and pattern your life. Because of Him, you are not alone. Because *[i]n the beginning was the Word, and the Word was with God, and the Word was God* (John 1:1)(KJV), you have the blueprint of the Bible to comfort your mind and guide you toward your path of righteousness.

Before I started to practice meditation on a regular basis, I saw a suggestion on social media about starting a "Gratefulness Jar." The concept was to get a jar and some index cards and write down at least one thing you were grateful for at the end of that day. I started the process on January 1, and at the end of the year on New Year's Eve, I opened each card and read it aloud. It was comforting to see how many cards I amassed over the year – it was many more than the 365-minimum. But even better than that, was the day-to-day remembrance that God blesses us with very small things each day. Some days I was merely grateful for the sunshine coming into my window. On other days, I was grateful for the smile from one of my children, or a kind word extended to me by a stranger.

During the negativity embodied in the demise of my marriage, I could reflect on the fact that there were still many good things happening around me, worthy of my continued "thanks." The process of writing them down helped me to renew my mind. It gave me an opportunity to focus on what was good, pure, and excellent in the process of taking back my life. By doing the exercise, I could let go of the attachment to some of my material desires–I had already lost a lucrative job, and was working in a call center trying to bounce back from my layoff. I was losing my marriage, losing my home, losing many of the things that I had worked hard to purchase, and losing the continuous company of my children every day of the year due to impending co-parenting. Whew!

As God would have it, being "forced" to be grateful helped me to soften my demeanor, and allowed me to open my heart and love people more fully. The practice helped me to see the brighter side of the things that were happening to me, and it also allowed me an opportunity to realize where some of my own choices had been the impetus for where I found myself at that point in my life. Writing out cards of gratefulness showed me that I could be content with less, and not constantly angry about what I had lost.

There's a reason why God admonishes us against vengeance: *Do not take revenge, my dear friends, but leave room for God's wrath, for it is written: "It is mine to avenge; I will repay," says the Lord.* Romans 12:19. (NIV) Spiteful retribution never comes from a positive mind-space. Taking matters into our own hands can extend the pain in our lives, and set us up for failure. Being grateful allowed me to see myself in a different light, and evaluate those choices. Simply put, being grateful helped me to let go of the mean-spirited person that many of us become when the rug is being pulled out from under our feet. With a renewed mind, my heart could yield to love – giving and receiving.

In order to take our lives back, we must dare to be different in our responses to negative stimuli. Take your life back by changing your mindset to extend love, grace and understanding even unto the broken person who tried to break you in one way or another. Extend an olive branch of forgiveness so that your mind is free to focus on the wonderful aspects of having a truly spiritual life.

Let go of the worldly desires and passions of the flesh that keep you tethered to the belief that you *need* more to BE more. Allow God the opportunity to minister to your heart by applying your mind to those pure and positive thoughts. It doesn't have to be all day, every day, to start. It can simply be seeing a negative situation for what it is, and instead of returning the negative energy, choosing to breathe through it; read through it; pray through it; speak to it,; or meditate on it, so that your true spiritual self shines through the moment.

We are all operating in moments of time. Break things down into smaller portions and you can connect your dots to a life of spiritual excellence – whatever that looks like to you. Change your mind and you will change your heart. Change your heart and you will change your environment. Change your environment and take your life back!

13 FREE TO CONFORM

What do we get by conforming to the expectations of others? We spend our lives trying to fit into this place, in one way or another for the good of the order, but why do we do it, and what does it get us? If we are on the job, we may curtail our boisterous personality so as not to accost others with our joviality, even if that happiness is being fueled by God. So instead of attending lunches, chatting at the water cooler or stepping into the boss' office, we hide behind a closed door under the pretense of producing some work product that just has to get done in that moment.

At home, we ride together in vehicles from place to place, shopping for groceries, picking up children, attending school functions. We clap, loudly as a collective with pride, speak as a unit to acquaintances, and parents of children who we recognize. We sit down at the table every night to family dinners of discussion and laughter. Engage in amplified discourse of politics and religion, and somehow agree to disagree. Climb into a warm bed where feet and legs touch, pass kisses and caresses across the invisible divide. Rise and fall, and close our eyes in prayer, left to our separate minds, and that is where REAL life begins.

I've learned that the facade is rarely what it seems. Everyone sees the grand building from a distance, but up close it's covered with grime from years of use and misuse, or a lack of care taking. When close, you can see the fault lines and cracks, the imperfections covered by the sparkle of glass, or the white-wash of a fresh coat of paint. Even worse, the building may suffer from inner sickness subject to more than just a surface repair. The air ducts might be clogged. Asbestos may cover the furnace, and all of the pipes throughout, and a good nick or two may eventually give way to a toxic environment. The problem is, you never know. One can never be sure what is underneath the surface of what stands in grand splendor.

And then you have God.

The one place where conformity brings nothing but joy. Where obedience to the Word only assists you in walking the path of the righteous. There are no ulterior motives in God's words. There are no attempts to control your actions by threat and fear. Trusting in God creates a total lack of fear. Bowing to His power to work in your life is 'fear' manifested as reverence.

I conform because I don't want to disappoint. I conform because I don't want to be left out. I conform because I want God to be happy with the person He created. I conform because I love my relationship with Him. Because the response is only geared toward what good I can accomplish for myself, not what the world believes I should be, to be accepted. Conforming to God's word allows us to reap benefits and rewards that no other human could ever produce. For man, it is always: "what have you done for me lately?" that keeps me in your presence. What have you got to give me in return? With God, the return you receive for obedience only serves to benefit you!

What have you done for yourself lately? *As obedient children, do not conform to the evil desires you had when you lived in ignorance. But just as he who called you is holy, so be holy in all you do; for it is written: "Be holy, because I am holy."* 1 Peter 1:14-16. (NIV) *Do not conform to the pattern of this world, but be transformed by the renewing of your mind. Then you will be able to test and approve what God's will is — his good, pleasing and perfect will.* Romans 12:2. (NIV)

I asked God in prayer: "Lord, make me over." He did, and I took my life back!

14 SPIRITUAL LOST AND FOUND

As your mind and heart begin to transform, your desires will change. You may want to take note of the changes by journaling your progress in some way. I realized how much my mind and heart changed several years ago the day I thought I lost my Bible:

This morning, I panicked! Why? Because I lost my Bible. Now, this may not seem like a problem for most and it shouldn't really be a problem for me: I have three Bible apps on my iPad, I have one Bible at my office, and my kids each have one of their own, so there is always a way to get to the Word.

But, nothing compares to My Bible.

This is the one that knows me! The one with all the underlines and markings of years of life-struggles to learn who I am, and where I need to be. The one that has the small pieces of paper with simple prayers for me ... things I need to be mindful of... people I need to remember. And of course, with every note in the side margin, I can reflect on where I was spiritually at the time, and on how much God has allowed me to grow just by putting myself in His presence.

And so, when I finished my morning prayers—which for this morning addressed my recent lack of spiritual focus—and went to pick up My Book, it wasn't where I thought it should be; where I tend to leave it. And I panicked. I mean, labored breathing; sinking stomach; mind racing; feet moving swiftly through each room. YOU KNOW THE FEELING! It's the same one you get when you can't find your keys, or your glasses, or your wallet, or your work product, or anything that you need in the moment to move you to the next process in your life—you can't make another move without it, and so you're stuck until it's located.

THAT feeling! I could never guess that the misplacement of a simple book could cause me such angst, but it did, and I'm glad! This was a quick morning lesson from my God to me. A quick intercession, so that I always remember to stay in the Word. A quick morning lesson on how I can't lose the focus of having Him at the forefront of my life. Tangible evidence that my mind, heart, needs, and desires have changed.

15 BE STRONG AND COURAGEOUS

SCRIPTURE 7: "Have I not commanded you? Be strong and courageous. Do not be afraid; do not be discouraged, for the LORD your God will be with you wherever you go." Joshua 1:9 (NIV)

More than anything, in order to take your life back you must have the strength to make a move, and the courage to keep it moving! You must become a leader over your own life, because God's promises are real. In Joshua 1:9, God *promises* to be where we go with one requirement. God says, *Have I not commanded you? Be strong and courageous. Do not be afraid; do not be discouraged, for the LORD your God will be with you wherever you go.* (NIV)

When we realize what gifts have been given to us by God, we recognize that there is a purpose on our life that requires us to take back its control from anything and anyone. However, we cannot move forward if we are fearful. Recall in Chapter 7 where I described the fear I felt every time I contemplated writing the Chapter on Zerubbabel and the rebuilding of the temple. Although God promised according to scripture to be with me on every page, instead of receiving His promise, I gave into the fear that the enemy put into my heart. I lacked strength, and I lacked courage to do what God had already ordained and anointed me to do the first day he began placing the focused scriptures on my mind, and the idea of the book in my heart. If God was so definitive as to give me the words and the way they should be used, why should I feel that He would not be with me whenever I sat down to type?

Without anything spiritual, we know how difficult it is to dig ourselves out of a rut, discard our lazy habits, and do what is required of us to take our lives to the next level. What Joshua tells us is that God requires us (He commands us by His word) to be strong and courageous, to face our fears, to not allow our disappointments to derail us. When we do that, God promises that wherever our strength and courage (even if minute and limited) takes us, He will be right there.

Becoming a Leader

Let's look for a minute at Joshua and see how our lives might compare. Joshua was not the original leader. Joshua was the number two guy, Moses' right-hand man. He was specifically qualified having followed Moses even without having the responsibility of complete leadership upon his shoulders.

Many times, we are in a position where we are established but not in the lead position. It does not mean that we are not capable of taking the lead. And it does not mean that what we are doing is not an important piece of the process. Often, God places us in position where we have the opportunity to look and learn, without the burden of responsibility, so that when our time comes, we are inherently capable of moving to the next level.

When Moses died, God anointed Joshua to take Moses' place and lead the Israelites into the land that God promised to their forefathers. The land was already promised, but still God needed to address and prepare the people for the fight before them. In Joshua 1:5, God told the Israelites, *"No one will be able to stand against you all the days of your life. As I was with Moses, so I will be with you; I will never leave you nor forsake you.* (NIV). The land was already promised, but a fight was going to ensue. Because of the promise, the Israelites should have known that God would be with them to help the promise be fulfilled.

As you read through the pages of this book, consider yourself Joshua. In your current state, you may not feel that you have much control over your own life circumstances. For many reasons, you may not have been the "leader" of your own physical or emotional person. Many times, we connect ourselves to people, places, things and jobs that because we have a certain need or reliance upon them (or it), we lack the confidence to take charge. We may be second in command of our own lives, sitting back and watching someone else call all of the shots, and make all of the moves. God promised it to you, but *you* must be wailing to occupy the land (your purpose-filled life).

Although you may not have been your own leader, the opportunity will present itself, and then, you will step into your own leadership role. This comes with understanding and believing that God did not give us a spirit of timidity or fear (2 Timothy 1:7). If God did not give us that spirit, then there is some other spiritual force operating against us, causing us to be shrinking violets when we should be nothing less than a cedar tree with the spirit of Christ within us.

As an aside, you may find it interesting to know that cedar trees can grow up to 100 feet tall and are common in areas with a good amount of rain. You should shout "Hallelujah!" right about now. This is why: *Then he prayed again, and heaven gave rain, and the earth bore its fruit.* James 5:18.(ESV) Every raindrop, obstacle, road block, diversion, closed door, heartache, disappointment is the rain you need to produce your fruit. *[S]o that you may be sons of your Father who is in heaven. For he makes his sun rise on the evil and on the good, and sends rain on the just and the unjust.* Matthew 5:45 (ESV). No one is immune, and that is a good thing! Your promise remains secure.

Strength to Move

"Courage" and "cowardice" both sound the same until the end. In your own life, have you ever received a promise from God about where you need to be, what you should be doing, and who you must be in order to see your promise fulfilled? Have you acted on those feelings with courageous movements toward your goal, or (like me) allowed your innate bravery to be squelched?

At one time or another, we have all felt that tiny "ping" in our stomachs, when an idea came across our mind, and feelings stirred in our spirit. For me, the ping told me to go on a solo cruise for my forty-fifth birthday and write my first novel. I knew it was the fulfillment of my promise as a writer because it was an idea that I could not dispel. My marriage was not doing well at the time. Trust issues caused my ex to question my motives for the cruise, even though I had expressed the idea to him many times before, and he assured me he was on-board. That was until it came time to purchase my ticket. At that moment he created such a disturbance in my spirit that I agreed with him and opted for us to take a cruise together – two months later.

There was no reason for me to believe that he was sincere about the cruise. His track record for honesty and follow-through was lacking when it came to me. But many times, out of fear and timidity, we unwillingly sacrifice our lives to other people who don't encourage our dreams, or who may have ulterior motives for sabotaging our lives. When this happens, we also lose our desire to manifest God's promises.

I never went on the cruise, and I never completed the journey to my first novel. My lack of belief in God's promise allowed me to rely on the promise of a man. I was too timid and fearful to stand up for what God shouted to my spirit, and instead hearkened to the tiny whisper of doubt from the devil. That is why managing your spiritual strength is paramount to taking your life back.

When we are not focused on our spiritual health, growth, and happiness, anything from eating a bowl of ice cream to taking your kids to yet another sporting or school related event, may be "used" to derail our process. Jesus reminds us that *[t]he thief comes only to steal and kill and destroy. I came that they may have life and have it abundantly*. John 10:10. (ESV) The devil comes in the form of *the* temptation that is most likely to derail *you*.

The devil knows our deceitful heart – he knows what we like and exactly how it needs to be packaged. Falling for the whispering that there is not enough time; you won't do a good job; no one will want to buy your product, etc., will have you paralyzed with fear. Indulging in our fleshly desires whether it be eating, drinking, relationships, or putting anything in our lives ahead of God, may prevent us from reaching our next level. The devil is our adversary, and he lays in wait for us to have second thoughts about what God means to us and wants for us. 1 Peter 5:8. Therefore, we must always seek wisdom through the Holy Spirit, maintaining our God-consciousness, and not be double-minded. James 1:5-7. We must be single-focused in a manner that will allow us to concentrate our efforts on building our relationship with God – brick-by-brick, stone-by-stone, firmly on the Rock and not on shifting sand. Matthew 7:24-27.

God's promise and favor are readily available. What God started in you will be finished. It is promised by God in James 1:5-6: 5. *because of your partnership in the gospel from the first day until now, 6. being confident of this, that he who began a good work in you will carry it on to completion until the day of Christ Jesus.* (NIV) God will not start a burning in your spirit that He has no intention to see through to completion. But in order to meet the requirements of our promise, we must rebuke the devil, and be in partnership with the gospel. In partnership with the gospel, we are then able to adhere to God's command that will ultimately assist you to take your life back. In doing so, you will bring others along with you: *"Be strong and courageous, because you will lead these people to inherit the land I swore to their ancestors to give them."* Joshua 1:6. (NIV)

Always remember that the reason for your gift is to share it with the people around you to God's glory. Because every good and perfect gift comes from above, when you put your gift to use in alignment with God, you not only take yourself to the promise land, but you help to lead others if they see you and say, "I want an anointing on my life like that one." Of course, no one can have *your* specific anointing, but the light that you emit, reflecting the image of God created by your relationship with Jesus Christ, may lead others to open their hearts and spiritual minds to accepting the anointing on their own lives.

"Be strong and very courageous. Be careful to obey all the law my servant Moses gave you; do not turn from it to the right or to the left, that you may be successful wherever you go." Joshua 1:7 (NIV)

Strength and courage come from being mindful of both God's precepts and His promises. As an example, if you start with the precept of forgiveness first, it can go a long way to building your inner strength because you free up the energy it takes to hold a grudge, frown, pout or pity yourself and the situation where you feel trapped. Releasing the energy to take revenge on the wrong-doer, and turning toward loving expressions (with all needed boundaries), allows us to smile when we used to cry. Everything we have ever needed to maneuver through this earthly existence, God has already placed inside of us. Therefore, we know that we have the courage to face our need to forgive. We need only turn to the scripture and meditate on its promise. *His divine power has given us everything we need for a godly life through our knowledge of him who called us by his own glory and goodness.* 2 Peter 1:3. (NIV) God would not give you an assignment that you were not capable of completing.

The struggles that you have encountered that led to your reading this book are everything you need in order to move your life forward. How so? When we go to the gym and begin to strength train, we utilize weights and repeat moves to various degrees. We tear our muscles and feel a momentary soreness until the healing begins, and the muscle grows. When the initial weights stop producing growth, we have to move on to a heavier weight, another tear, momentary soreness and continued growth. Unfortunately, life seems to work in the same way. As Bishop T.D. Jakes once said, "We don't lift weights to change the weights." The weight is purposed to fine tune our bodies, and when the weights are emotional, they are used to build our character, integrity, and our faith. Each time we face a setback, and strive to make a comeback, we are strengthened in these areas. As we build our relationship with God, eventually, the time it takes to recover from the tearing should be less, and the growth should make us stronger.

Do not shy away from your past derailments. In Christ there is no shame and no condemnation. Instead, take a prayerful opportunity to look at them, dissect them and apply any one of the seven scriptures to your issue. *1. Therefore, there is now no condemnation for those who are in Christ Jesus, 2. because through Christ Jesus the law of the Spirit who gives life has set you free from the law of sin and death.* Romans 8:1-2 (NIV). Meditate on the scriptural solution in your quiet time, and literally ask God for clarity. Ask God for wisdom for the best way to use your gift to strengthen your approach. As you build strength, you build confidence, and the courage to prepare to cross over to your promises and take your life back for good! … *And surely I am with you always, to the very end of age.* Matthew 28:20 (NIV)

The Beginning . . .

16 CONCLUSION

I pray every day.

I'm not sure that I always prayed every day, but I'm sure that I do now. I don't always get on my knees, but God is almost always on my mind and in my heart.

I'm not overtly pious. I make what many people would consider spiritual and religious "mistakes." Well, I'll be damn, I am human. I hope that made you laugh

Life is a funny business, and even your spirituality can be a source of great humor – I believe that God showed Himself to have a sense of humor simply by the way men and women are wired so differently that we may never really understand one another without God's intervention, and even then we may still fail one another. Maybe that's why He wired us so differently and yet, made us feel as if we needed one another to really get by. Maybe he wanted us to be in a position where we would need to confer with Him every day, for everything imaginable, and then some things that we cannot even fathom.

SPEAK THE WORD!

And so, I pray:

Thank you Father for this day.
Thank you for the sun, the moon, and the stars.
Thank you for separating darkness from light.
Thank you for giving us light in darkness so that we are always reminded that we have a way back to You.
Thank you for every bird that flies in the sky.
Thank you for everything that walks, crawls, slithers, hops, and jumps on the earth.
Thank you for the seed and the fruit.
Thank you, Father for every creature in the sea – from the smallest amoeba to the largest whale; and
Thank you Father for giving man dominion over all things in the earth – to walk as a perfect reflection of you; to show our kindness, our grace, our mercy, our strength, our power, our love through Jesus Christ.
Love fulfills the law:
Keep us ever so mindful that Love is patient and kind, it does not envy, or boast, it does not dishonor others, it is not self-seeking; it keeps no record of wrongs; Love does not rejoice in iniquity but rejoices in the truth; it always protects, always trusts, always hopes, always believes; always endures. Love never fails.
Thank you, Father for every raindrop, every snowflake, every blade of grass.
Thank you for every drop of water that makes up the ocean and every grain of sand that makes up the desert.
Thank you for every mountain high and valley low.
Thank you Father that when we come upon these things and wonder: "How could something so big come from something so small; how could something so small make something so big?"
We know Father that the answer is you.
And so we thank you for every tree, every leaf, every flower, every petal, ever fragrance.
We thank you for every color in the spectrum, and

We thank you for our five senses plus the Holy Spirit to enjoy life abundantly as you planned.

We thank you for being the Big Plan seer.

For sitting high and looking low.

For being the Alpha and the Omega.

The author and finisher of our lives.

We thank you Father that before we were fashioned in our mother's wombs you knew us.

And because you knew us, you had a plan for us.

A plan for us to do well and prosper, to have hope and a future.

We thank you Father that if we seek ye first the Kingdom of heaven and its righteousness, all other things will come unto us.

We thank you that if we humble ourselves under your mighty hand, casting all our cares to you because you love us, that even if we are down for a while, in due time you will exalt us.

Amen!

This book, I hope, encompasses my entire prayer.

ABOUT THE AUTHOR

Khairiya Charlyne Bryant (Khai-Missy) was born and raised in Roosevelt, (Long Island), New York, to Charles and Dorothy Stewart Bryant. She is the youngest of five children, and mother of the Magnificent Seven. Khairiya graduated from Roosevelt Jr. Sr. High School in Roosevelt, NY, at the age of 16. She attended Howard University, where she was a member of the HU Marching Bison Band, T-Phi-M, Tau Beta Sigma National Honorary Band Sorority, and a reporter for The Hilltop.

After starting her family, she completed her schooling at Florida State University, where she received her Bachelor of Arts in English, concentrating in Creative Writing. She attended the Florida State University College of Law while raising five children, and received her Juris Doctorate as a member of the class of 2005.

While she remains a licensed member of the Florida Bar, Khairiya currently resides in Greenville, South Carolina with the last three of her seven children, and has been an active church member of Redemption, under Pastor Ron Carpenter, Jr., since 2015. Prior to her move to Greenville, she lived in Tallahassee, Florida and attended Tabernacle Missionary Baptist Church under Pastor Reverend Stanley L. Walker.

Khairiya will release a book of poetry (Love Puddles) and her first novel (How Many Scoops?) in the near future.

Made in the USA
Columbia, SC
20 November 2017